WALKER BOOKS

This
Nature Storybook
belongs to:

First published 2009 by Walker Books Ltd

87 Vauxhall Walk, London SE11 5HJ

This edition published 2015

10 9 8 7 6 5 4 3 2 1

Text © 2009 Steve Voake

Illustrations © 2009 Charlotte Voake

The rights of Steve Voake and Charlotte Voake to be identified as author
and illustrator respectively of this work has been asserted by them in
accordance with the Copyright, Designs and Patents Act 1988.

This book has been typeset in Godlike and Charlotte

Printed in China

British Library Cataloguing
in Publication Data: a catalogue record
for this book is available from the British Library

ISBN 978-1-4063-6689-1

www.walker.co.uk

WALKER BOOKS
AND SUBSIDIARIES
LONDON • BOSTON • SYDNEY • AUCKLAND

For Tory
S. V.

INSECT DETECTIVE

Steve Voake

ILLUSTRATED BY

CHARLOTTE VOAKE

RIGHT now, all around you,
thousands of insects are doing strange
and wonderful things.
But you can't always
see them straight away.

Sometimes you have to know
where to look…

THERE
ARE MORE
INSECTS LIVING IN
THE WORLD THAN ALL
THE OTHER ANIMALS PUT
TOGETHER – THAT'S ABOUT
200 MILLION INSECTS FOR EVERY
SINGLE PERSON!

LISTEN – just by the fence –
can you hear a scratching sound?
A wasp is scraping away at
the post with her strong jaws.
She's collecting wood.

She mixes it into a soft pulp
in her mouth and when she has
enough, she'll help the other wasps
build a nest out of paper.

WASPS OFTEN COLLECT DIFFERENT SORTS OF WOOD, WHICH MAKES THEIR NESTS LOOK STRIPY – JUST LIKE THE INSECTS WHO MADE THEM!

Not all kinds
of wasps live together,
but lots of them do.

INSECTS THAT LIVE TOGETHER ARE CALLED "SOCIAL INSECTS".

Ants *always* live together.

They usually make their nests underground.

Finding an ants' nest is easy:

FIRST find an ant ...

then follow it.

It might stop to chat with some other
ants along the way (ants
can communicate
by touching their
antennae
together) ...

but after a while,
the ant will head for home
and you'll be able to
find out where it lives.

LIKE ALL INSECTS,
ANTS HAVE THREE MAIN
BODY PARTS.

THORAX

ABDOMEN

HEAD

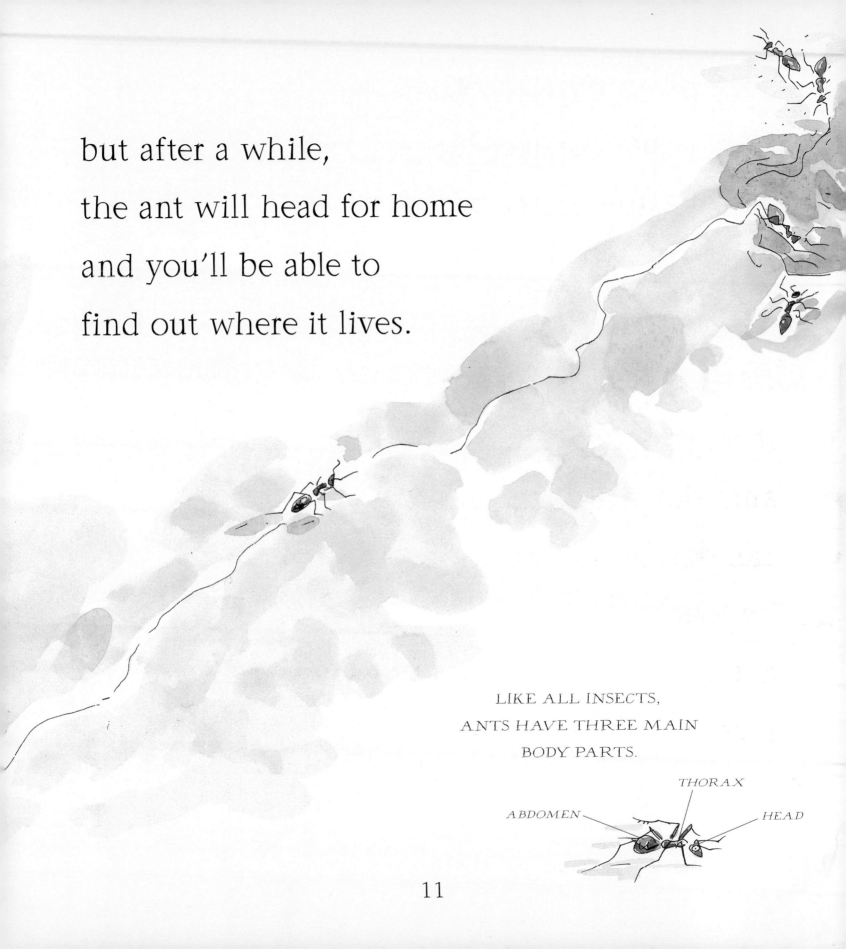

Solitary bees live by themselves ("solitary" means alone). This female solitary bee is busy collecting food from the spring flowers. She'll store it in her tiny nest, ready for when her eggs hatch out.

ALL
INSECTS
START
LIFE AS
EGGS.

12

Solitary bees make their
nests in holes in the ground,
cracks in walls or in tiny
cavities that have been left
by other insects.

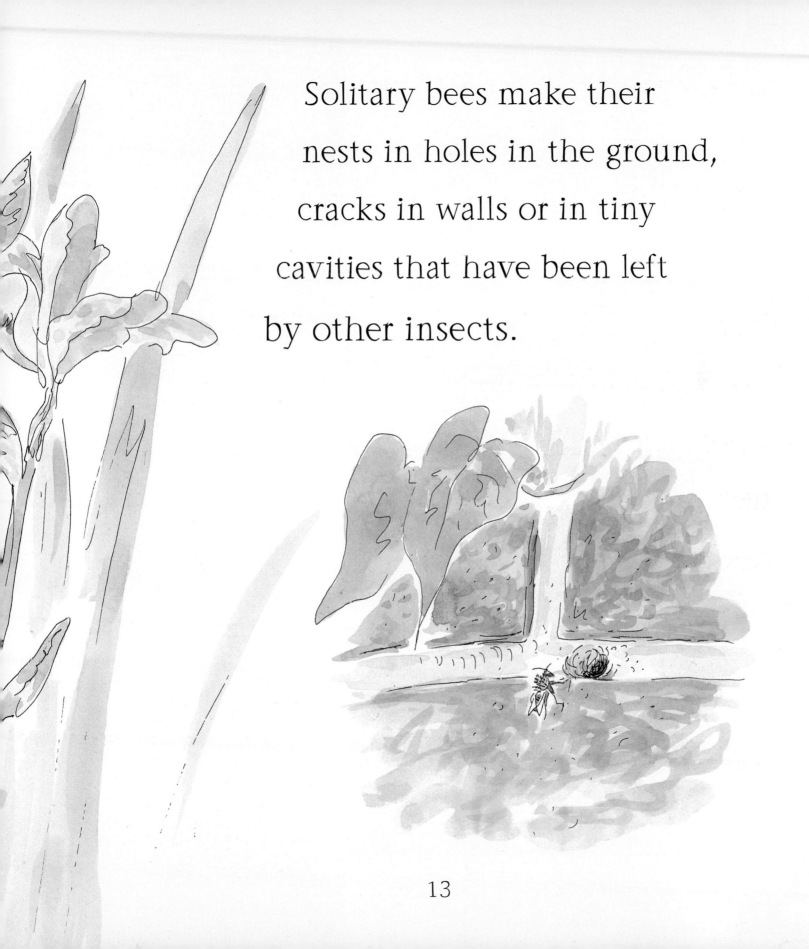

Plenty of animals like to eat insects
for dinner. So some insects use camouflage
to blend in with their surroundings.

Look at this crinkly
brown leaf. Can you
see a crinkly brown
Herald moth too?

They often rest in trees during the day
so that birds won't see them.

Insects have other
ways of hiding too.
See the squiggly
lines on these leaves?
They were made by
a leaf-miner caterpillar.
The leaf-miner protects
itself by living between
the top and bottom
layers of leaves –
a bit like
hiding in
a sandwich!

15

Lift up a stone ... you might see

an earwig scuttle out. They like

to hide in the damp and the dark.

The pincers on the tips of their abdomens

make them look rather fierce,

but don't worry – they're

completely harmless.

FEMALE EARWIGS ARE VERY GOOD MOTHERS. THEY WORK HARD TO KEEP THEIR EGGS CLEAN, TURNING AND WASHING THEM REGULARLY. WHEN THE YOUNG HATCH, THEIR MOTHERS BRING THEM FOOD UNTIL THEY'RE OLD ENOUGH TO LOOK AFTER THEMSELVES.

Of course, you *might* find
some creatures under there
which aren't insects:

spiders,

centipedes,

woodlice,

slugs ...

and once I found a
baby frog!

It's easy to
tell whether
something is
an insect or not.

All you have to do is count the legs.

1, 2, 3, 4, 5, 6 —

If it's got SIX legs, it's an insect.

If it hasn't ... it isn't!

If you're lucky, you
might even find
a violet ground beetle, gleaming in the
sunlight. It's like discovering a precious jewel!

But ground beetles aren't just lovely to look at, they're excellent hunters too. At night they go out hunting for slugs and snails, which makes gardeners very happy!

Perhaps the greatest insect
hunter of all is the dragonfly.
Even the name sounds fierce!

But don't worry – they won't come
chasing after you. Dragonflies are much
more interested in catching
things like bluebottles,
mosquitoes and
midges. Some will
even snatch a spider
from its web.

On summer days when the air is still, you can see their wings sparkling in the light as they hunt, twisting, diving and plucking flies from the air.

DRAGONFLIES ARE FABULOUS FLIERS; THEY HAVE TWO SETS OF POWERFUL WINGS, WHICH THEY CAN USE TO HOVER, CHANGE DIRECTION AND EVEN TO FLY BACKWARDS.

It's hard to believe they started life in the water ...

but dragonflies lay their eggs in ponds
or slow-moving rivers, where they hatch out
into small dragonfly "nymphs".

A nymph sheds its skin many times until
it is fully grown. Finally it climbs out of the
water and rests on the stem of a plant. As
dawn breaks, its skin splits open and a
beautiful dragonfly emerges, unfolding
its wings and drying itself in the sun.

THE SPECIAL CHANGES THAT TAKE PLACE IN INSECTS' BODIES
ARE CALLED "METAMORPHOSES". THEY HAPPEN IN DIFFERENT
WAYS, AS INSECTS GROW FROM EGGS TO ADULTS.

Sometimes, when you think about these strange and wonderful things – moths hiding, ants talking, dragonflies changing – it's hard to believe that they could really be true.

But you don't have to take my word for it ...

all you have to do is open the door
and step outside.

BE AN INSECT DETECTIVE!

Find out which beetles live near you by burying a jam jar in the earth. Any beetles walking over the top during the night will fall in. But remember to check every morning and let them go when you have finished looking.

When it gets dark, put a camping light on a white sheet outside. This will attract moths and you will be able to get a really close look at them!

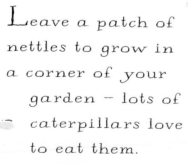

Leave a patch of nettles to grow in a corner of your garden – lots of caterpillars love to eat them. How many can you find?

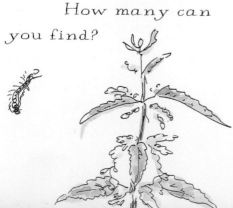

Try making a place for solitary bees to live. Rinse out an empty tin can, put some glue (or melted wax) in the bottom and fill it with drinking straws. Then hang the can up with the straws pointing slightly downwards to prevent rain collecting in them. When spring arrives, you'll soon see a few bees coming along to investigate!

28

Flying can be hard work for bumble-bees. If you see one crawling around on the ground, it may have run out of energy.

Mix some sugar and water in a teaspoon and give the bee a drink –

it will soon be busy among the flowers again!

Take a close look at wooden tables, fences or benches you see outside. If they have tiny lines all over them, you'll know a wasp has been there before you.

In hot thundery weather, keep an eye out for swarming ants. When the temperature is just right, the young queens will be brought up to the surface ready to mate and fly away to make new colonies.

INDEX

Look up the pages to find out about all these insect things. Don't forget to look at both kinds of words –

this kind

and

THIS KIND.

Note to Parents

Sharing books with children is one of the best ways to help them learn. And it's one of the best ways they learn to read, too.

Nature Storybooks are beautifully illustrated, award-winning information picture books whose focus on animals has a strong appeal for children. They can be read as stories, revisited and enjoyed again and again, inviting children to become excited about a subject, to think and discover, and to want to find out more.

Each book is an adventure into the real world that broadens children's experience and develops their curiosity and understanding — and that's the best kind of learning there is.

Note to Teachers

Nature Storybooks provide memorable reading experiences for children in Key Stages 1 and 2 (Years 1–4), and also offer many learning opportunities for exploring a topic through words and pictures.

By working with the stories, either individually or together, children can respond to the animal world through a variety of activities, including drawing and painting, role play, talking and writing.

The books provide a rich starting-point for further research and for developing children's knowledge of information genres.

Nature Storybooks support the literacy curriculum in a variety of ways, providing:

- a focus for a whole class topic
- high-quality texts for guided reading
- a resource for the class read-aloud programme
- information texts for the class and school library for developing children's individual reading interests

Find more information on how to use Nature Storybooks in the classroom at
www.walker.co.uk/naturestorybooks

Nature Storybooks support KS 1–2 English and KS 1–2 Science